the Seminole

The First People of Florida

by Mary Englar

Consultant:
Emman Spain
Historic Preservation Office
Seminole Nation of Oklahoma
Wewoka, Oklahoma

Bridgestone Books

an imprint of Capstone Press
Mankato, Minnesota

Bridgestone Books are published by Capstone Press
151 Good Counsel Drive • P.O. Box 669 • Mankato, Minnesota 56002
http://www.capstone-press.com

Printed in the United States of America.

Library of Congress Cataloging-in-Publication Data
Englar, Mary.
  The Seminole: The First People of Florida / by Mary Englar.
       p. cm.—(American Indian Nations)
  Summary: Provides an overview of the past and present lives of the
  Seminole people of Florida and Oklahoma, covering their customs and
  beliefs, government, and more.
  Includes bibliographical references and index.
  ISBN 0-7368-1358-6 (hardcover)
  1. Seminole Indians—Juvenile literature. [1. Seminole Indians. 2. Indians
  of North America—Southern states.] I. Title. II. Series.
  E99.S28 E54 2002
  975.9004'973—dc21   2002000011

Editorial Credits
Charles Pederson, editor; Kia Adams, designer and illustrator; Deirdre Barton,
photo researcher; Karen Risch, product planning editor

Photo Credits
Marilyn "Angel" Wynn, cover, cover inset, 4, 17, 22, 32, 35, 41, 44, 45; Capstone
Press Archives/Distributors of Florida, 8; Hulton/Archive, 11; PhotoDisc, 12–13;
Capstone Press/Gary Sundermeyer, 13; Hulton/Archive by Getty Images, 14;
International Stock, 16; Bettmann/CORBIS, 18; Artville, LLC, 19; North Wind
Picture Archives, 20, 25; Stock Montage, Inc., 27; Lost Tribes.Net/Theodore
Morris, 28; CORBIS/Keystone View Company, 30; Archives & Manuscripts
Division of Oklahoma Historical Society, 36; Lake County Museum/CORBIS,
38; Associated Press, AP, 42–43

1 2 3 4 5 6 07 06 05 04 03 02

Table of Contents

Features

George Billie is wearing a colorful Seminole jacket. He is a Florida Seminole. The Florida Seminole live on six reservations. Many other Seminole live in Oklahoma.

Chapter One

Who Are the Seminole?

The Seminole Indians sometimes have been called the "unconquered people." Today, about 13,800 Seminole live in southern Oklahoma and Florida.

About 60 percent of the people in the Seminole Nation of Oklahoma live in Seminole County southeast of Oklahoma City. Their headquarters is at Wewoka, Oklahoma. The rest of the Oklahoma Seminole live across Oklahoma and the United States.

The Florida Seminole tribes are divided into three groups. These groups are the Seminole tribe of Florida, the Independent Seminole, and the Miccosukee Tribe. These groups live on six reservations that the U.S. government has set aside for the Seminole to use. The reservations include Fort Pierce, Big Cypress, Immokalee, Brighton, Hollywood, and Tampa Reservations.

The Muskogee Indian ancestors of the Seminole lived in Alabama and Georgia. The Muskogee are sometimes called "Creek." In the early 1700s, many Muskogee began to move into northern Florida. Eventually, they became independent of the Muskogee in Alabama and Georgia. The Spanish called the Florida Muskogee *cimarrónes*, or "free people."

By the 1770s, the Muskogee had adopted the word *cimarrónes* into their language. They pronounced the word "Seminole" because their language had no *r* sound. They began to call themselves "Seminole." Today, the Oklahoma Seminole speak the Muskogee language. The Seminole of Florida speak Muskogee, Miccosukee, or both. Most Seminole also speak English.

The Seminole people continue to live their lives in their own way. They are proud of their culture and history. They fight to protect their land and way of life. They respect nature and work to protect it.

Seminole Lands

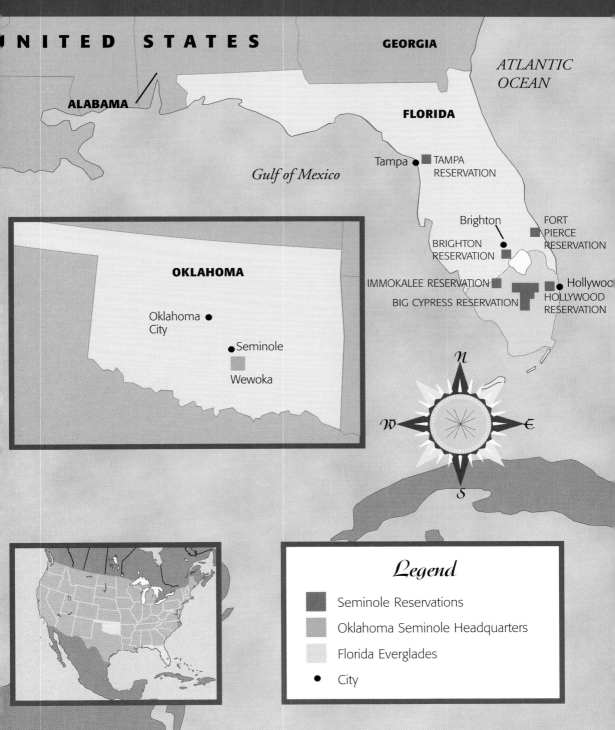

UNITED STATES

GEORGIA

ATLANTIC OCEAN

ALABAMA

FLORIDA

Gulf of Mexico

Tampa ● ■ TAMPA RESERVATION

Brighton
■ FORT PIERCE RESERVATION
BRIGHTON RESERVATION ●

IMMOKALEE RESERVATION ■

BIG CYPRESS RESERVATION

■ Hollywood
HOLLYWOOD RESERVATION

OKLAHOMA

Oklahoma ●
City

● Seminole
■
Wewoka

N
W E
S

Legend

■ Seminole Reservations

■ Oklahoma Seminole Headquarters

■ Florida Everglades

● City

A Seminole family creates traditional Seminole
corn dolls and other crafts.

Chapter Two

Traditional Life

Northern Florida is similar to the Alabama and Georgia land that the Muskogee left. It is hilly, with many forests, lakes, and rivers. In Florida, the Muskogee found good land to farm. They also found wild deer, turkeys, ducks, and bears to hunt.

The Muskogee kept many of their Georgia and Alabama traditions. For example, they built villages along the rivers and lived in log homes. They traded with the Spanish and with other American Indian nations.

In the early 1700s, Spain claimed the northern Florida area where some Muskogee moved. Increasing numbers of white European settlers pushed the Muskogee out of Georgia and Alabama. The Muskogee began to believe they were losing their traditional lands to the settlers.

The Importance of Trade

Deer were important to the Seminole. Hunters killed deer and prepared them for food. Women and children then cleaned and dried the deerskins. The Seminole used the skins for clothing and for trade.

During the 1700s and 1800s, the most important trading partners of the Seminole were the Spanish. The Seminole traded deerskins for items they wanted from the Spanish. Good hunters could trade about 40 pounds (18 kilograms) of deerskins each year. They traded for knives, buckles, guns, bullets, and tools. They also traded for glass bottles, silver jewelry, glass beads, and cloth.

Gathering and Preparing Foods

The Seminole people worked hard for food. The women and girls tended gardens of corn, melons, squash, beans, and other

The Seminole used spears and canoes to catch fish.

vegetables. The men cared for cattle and pigs and also hunted. Male relatives taught the young boys to hunt and fish. The men and boys trapped small game animals such as rabbits and birds. They used bows and arrows to hunt larger game such as deer. The Seminole used turkey feathers for the arrows and carved arrowheads from fish bones.

All villagers tended larger fields of crops. They harvested and stored these crops for later use. The most important Seminole crop was corn. Each family gave a part of its crops to be stored. Anyone who needed food later could use the stored food.

The women and girls prepared meals using vegetables from the gardens. They also used wild berries and plants. The Seminole made many dishes from corn. Sofki is a traditional hot soup of soaked and stewed corn. Seminole still eat sofki today.

Women and girls gathered and washed a wild plant called coontie. They crushed the coontie roots with wooden tools, put them in a basket, and soaked them in water. They strained the water through a cloth and allowed it to dry. They used the starch left behind to produce flour to make small cakes.

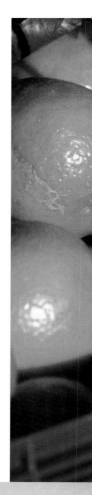

Seminole Honey Oranges

In the early 1500s, Spanish explorers visited Florida. They brought Seville oranges with them on their sailing ships. This fruit added vitamin C to their diet while they were at sea. Seville oranges were sour and tasted more like lemons than like oranges of today. Seeds from this fruit were dropped or planted in Florida, and the Seminole people began to gather and eat the fruit. Adding a bit of lemon juice to the recipe makes the oranges taste more like the original Seville fruit.

Ingredients:
4 oranges
4 teaspoons (20 mL) honey
½ teaspoon (2.5 mL) lemon juice

Equipment:
sharp kitchen knife
grapefruit spoon
small bowl
measuring spoons
mixing spoon

What you do:
1. With adult supervision, use the sharp kitchen knife to cut off the top one-third of each orange.
2. Use a grapefruit spoon to remove pieces of the orange fruit without cutting or poking through the orange peel.
3. Place orange pieces and juice into the small bowl.
4. When the inside of each orange and orange top is hollow, set aside the pieces.
5. Add honey and lemon juice to orange pieces and juice in bowl.
6. Mix gently with a spoon.
7. Use the spoon to replace orange sections and juice into the empty orange shells.
8. Replace the tops on the filled oranges and let them sit for 4 hours at room temperature before serving.

Makes 4 servings

A Florida Seminole family displayed their pottery in this 1974 photo.
The family made the pottery to use at home and to sell to tourists.

Family Roles

Seminole villages were organized around family clans. These groups of related people descended from a female ancestor. Children always belonged to their mother's clan. The home, animals, and crops belonged to the women. Clan names such as Alligator, Beaver, Bird, Wind, Snake, and Potato came from features of the natural world. The largest clan today is the Panther Clan.

Seminole children learned to work around the village at a young age. Young girls tended crops, prepared food, and took care of younger children. They learned to weave baskets and sew. Boys spent hours learning how to hunt and fish. They often used bows and arrows.

Boys became adults at age 12. Girls became adults at age 14. Young people always married someone from another clan. Two people from the same clan were considered to be related and could not marry each other.

The young woman's clan leader had to approve the marriage. Older members of the clan looked at the young man's ability to provide for a wife and family. They looked at the young woman's ability to run a home. Once the marriage was approved, the couple was married during a religious event such as the Green Corn Ceremony. Ceremonies are traditional dances or prayers that celebrate important events.

The Seminole believed that everything, including birds and trees, had spirits.

Traditional Beliefs

Seminole believed that spirits lived in everything. There were spirits in the earth, sun, moon, stars, animals, and trees.

Most Seminole villages had a medicine man. This person's position was important in the village. The medicine man studied wild plants. He gathered the plants and some animal bones into a medicine bundle. The medicine man used the bundles in ceremonies to heal sick people.

The medicine man chose younger village members to study to become medicine men. The young boys had to study at least seven years. Some studied as long as 20 years to become medicine men.

Medicine man Bobby Henry sings at a Seminole ceremony. He keeps rhythm with a rattle.

Ceremonies

The Seminole held many ceremonies during the year. They thanked the spirits for a good harvest, a good hunt, or good weather. The ceremonies honored nature's gifts from the spirits.

The most important ceremony was the Green Corn Ceremony. The medicine man chose the date for the start of the ceremony. It usually took place when the first corn was ripe. The ceremony lasted from four to eight days. Young boys between the ages of 13 and 15 often received a new name from the medicine man during these ceremonies.

Ceremonies such as this wedding were important to the Seminole. Weddings often took place during the Green Corn Ceremony.

Green Corn Ceremony

The Seminole tribes shared the Green Corn Ceremony. This ceremony celebrated the first ripe corn of the year. It was a time for the people to heal themselves and come together with their clans. The ceremony sometimes is called "busk." This name comes from a Muskogee word, *baskita,* which means "to fast." The Seminole believed that not eating food would clean their bodies and spirits.

To start the new season fresh, people replaced broken pots, made new clothes, and cleaned their houses and public buildings. On court day, people brought reports of crime to the older men of the village. After hearing from everyone involved, the men made a judgment. All past debts were paid, and people forgave each other for wrongs they had done.

After four to eight days of fasting, the villagers prepared a large meal. Everyone ate and danced to celebrate the new year. They played ball games.

Today, the Florida Seminole still celebrate the Green Corn Ceremony. The time is kept secret from outsiders, so only Seminole can attend. Many people return to the village to visit with their clans. The ceremony might include hours of stomp dancing. In this type of dancing, the people follow in a line behind a medicine man. The medicine man sings, and the men answer him. The women tie rattles to their legs to keep the rhythm. The villages still hold a court day to settle problems.

The Oklahoma Seminole also celebrate the Green Corn Ceremony. Their ceremony is also secret and lasts four days. They drink a liquid made from the roots of a pussy willow. They have dances that the Florida Seminole do not have. The Oklahoma Seminole do not have a court day.

The Seminole lived in Florida for many years. In the 1800s, U.S. settlers began to move onto their lands.

20

Chapter Three

The Seminole Wars

After the U.S. Revolutionary War (1775–1783) ended, more Europeans came to the United States. Many new settlers pushed into traditional Seminole lands in the Southeast. More American Indians moved into Spanish Florida to get away from the settlers.

In the early 1800s, many conflicts occurred between the Seminole and U.S. settlers near the Georgia and Alabama border with Spanish Florida. The settlers believed that the Spanish did not punish the Seminole for raiding American ranches and stealing cattle. The settlers decided to

Chickees

When the Seminole moved south to avoid U.S. settlers and soldiers, they left behind their traditional log houses. They began to build open-sided houses called chickees. The Seminole built chickees and quickly could leave them to escape U.S. soldiers.

The Seminole built chickees with materials from the palmetto tree. Palmetto trunks were straight and made good poles. The Seminole set four to eight palmetto poles into the ground. They then wove the fan-shaped leaves into a roof. Finally, they attached a platform of palmetto logs to the poles about 3 feet (1 meter) off the ground.

The open sides let the breeze move through the chickee. Southern Florida was much warmer than northern Florida, and the breezes helped the people stay cool. The platform kept belongings out of the water that sometimes flooded Seminole camps. The people slept on the platforms. They hung food, clothing, and deerskins from the poles that held up the roof.

Chickees continue to be popular in Florida. Many Seminole build chickees for their neighbors who are not Seminole. The chickees provide shade next to swimming pools and harbors. Some people use the chickees to cover backyard patio furniture or outdoor grills. The chickees still have palmetto leaf roofs, but cypress logs sometimes are used for the poles.

punish the Seminole for the raids. The settlers looted Seminole villages and kidnapped and killed Seminole people. The settlers also stole Seminole cattle.

Many African American slaves from the United States also crossed into Florida to escape slavery. The slave owners often mistreated the slaves. The African Americans learned that if they ran away to Florida, Spain would not force them to return.

The Seminole welcomed many escaped African Americans. They were good farmers and ranchers. They built their own towns near those of the Seminole. Some African Americans married Seminole and learned to speak Seminole languages. These African American Freedmen fought with the Seminole against U.S. soldiers. The Seminole accepted the Freedmen as allies, or friends, but not as members of the Seminole nation. After 1866, the U.S. government forced the Oklahoma Seminole to make the Freedmen citizens of the tribe.

The First Seminole War

When the settlers began to cross into northern Florida, the Seminole moved into the swamps of southern Florida. In 1817, General Andrew Jackson illegally led 2,000 U.S. soldiers into Florida. He wanted to stop raids on American farms and to return escaped slaves to their U.S. owners. Even more, Jackson wanted to force Spain to give up its claim to Florida.

For about two years, Jackson's troops fought the First Seminole War (1817–1819). The troops burned Seminole villages and chased the people toward the swamps of southern Florida.

By 1821, Spain realized it could not protect its Florida lands from the United States. Spain signed the Adams-Onis Treaty, which sold Florida to the United States. The United States agreed to repay Spain up to $5 million for damages that Spanish settlers in Florida suffered during the fighting. The U.S. government also agreed to drop claims to Texas, which Spain owned. Florida became a U.S. territory in 1822.

More Problems with Settlers

As settlers moved into Florida from surrounding states, they often settled on traditional Seminole land. In 1823, some Seminole leaders signed the Treaty of Moultrie Creek with the U.S. government. Seminole leaders agreed to give up all their land in northern Florida and move to a reservation in central Florida. In return, the U.S. government promised to build schools, protect the reservation from settlers, and provide food for one year.

Many Seminole did not agree to the treaty's terms. They claimed that the leaders who signed the agreement did not represent all Seminole. This group did not want to move. They considered the land in central Florida too swampy for farming.

In 1830, the U.S. Congress passed the Indian Removal Act by one vote. This law allowed the U.S. president to force southeastern American Indians onto land west of the Mississippi River. This land in present-day Oklahoma was called Indian Territory. When the Indian nations were gone, the U.S. government took over their lands for settlers.

In the drawing above, Seminole warriors prepare to attack U.S. soldiers. Seminole warriors fought against U.S. soldiers during the First Seminole War.

The Second Seminole War

In 1831, a period of dry weather ruined Seminole crops, and the Seminole were hungry. The U.S. government offered Seminole leaders food if they moved west to the Indian Territory. Some leaders signed the Treaty of Payne's Landing and prepared to move. But other Seminole were angry. They said that they would fight before giving up their land in Florida.

In December 1835, three Seminole leaders led a band of several hundred warriors. The leaders' names were Micanopy, Jumper, and Alligator. Their warriors attacked a group of 108 U.S. soldiers, killing all but two. The event set off the Second Seminole War (1835–1842). The attack convinced the U.S. government to send more troops to fight the Seminole.

Osceola, Micanopy, and others led the war. The Seminole often ambushed the soldiers, hiding along trails to attack. After an attack, the Seminole disappeared into the forests and swamps of central and southern Florida. The Seminole knew the swamps better than the soldiers did. The soldiers were afraid to chase the Seminole into the swamps. If the soldiers did find them, the Seminole could quickly move their camps.

The U.S. soldiers were unsure how to capture the Seminole and end the war. They decided to burn Seminole villages and destroy their crops. They killed the Seminole cattle and stole

Osceola

In 1804, the Seminole leader Osceola was born in the Muskogee town of Tallahassee. This town was near present-day Tuskegee, Alabama. Osceola's name means "black drink crier." He was known for his ability to drink the strong black tea used for Seminole religious ceremonies.

Osceola's father was a British trader named William Powell. His mother was a Seminole woman named Polly Copinger. The family of Osceola's mother moved to Florida to escape the conflicts between the Seminole and U.S. settlers. In 1835, some Seminole left Florida for Indian Territory. Osceola refused to leave.

The Seminole and the soldiers who fought them found Osceola to be a brave warrior. He led many raids against U.S. troops. Although outnumbered, the Seminole used ambush to fight the soldiers. After attacking from a hiding place, the Seminole hid in the swamps.

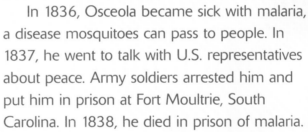

In 1836, Osceola became sick with malaria, a disease mosquitoes can pass to people. In 1837, he went to talk with U.S. representatives about peace. Army soldiers arrested him and put him in prison at Fort Moultrie, South Carolina. In 1838, he died in prison of malaria.

Osceola is the best known of all Seminole warriors. Counties and towns all over the United States are named for him. His death inspired the Seminole to continue fighting for several years. His grave is near the entrance to Fort Moultrie National Monument on Sullivan's Island, South Carolina.

their horses. The soldiers sometimes captured a Freedman. When that happened, the soldiers promised not to return him to slavery if he revealed the location of the Seminole camps. By 1842, most of the Seminole and Freedmen were living in Indian Territory.

The Second Seminole War lasted seven years and cost the United States more than $20 million. It was the longest and most expensive of wars against American Indians.

Billy Bowlegs was a Seminole chief. For years, he refused to surrender during the Third Seminole War.

After the war, fewer than 500 Seminole Indians lived in Florida. They hid in Big Cypress Swamp and in the Everglades. The soldiers could not search this large, swampy area of southern Florida. For several years, the Seminole lived in peace.

The Third Seminole War

Settlers continued to move even farther south into Florida, which became a state in 1845. The remaining Seminole again fought with settlers in the Third Seminole War (1855–1858). The U.S. government wanted the last Seminole to leave Florida peacefully. The government invited Chief Billy Bowlegs to Washington, D.C. The government wanted him to see how large the United States had become.

Bowlegs refused to leave Florida. U.S. soldiers found and burned his camp in 1857. They took the stored corn and rice. Bowlegs knew he could not continue fighting without food and a place to live. In 1858, Bowlegs and 164 Seminole left for Indian Territory.

By the end of the three Seminole Wars, only about 150 Seminole remained in Florida. Thousands had been forced into Indian Territory. Many of these Seminole died of starvation and disease while waiting to be moved. Others died because of poor conditions on the trip to Indian Territory.

Seminole family members wear traditional patchwork clothing in this 1926 photo. Modern Seminole often wear patchwork.

Chapter Four

Modern Seminole

After the Seminole Wars, the lives of the
Seminole people of Florida and Oklahoma
became different from each other. The
people continued to share some traditions,
but each group also developed its own
government and traditions.

The Florida Seminole

For 40 years, the remaining Florida
Seminole hid in Big Cypress Swamp and
the Everglades. They raised cattle, pigs, and
chickens. They planted corn on dry islands

Seminole Patchwork

Patchwork clothing is one of the best-known Seminole crafts. Making patchwork has become a Seminole cultural tradition. Beginning in the late 1800s, Seminole women sewed colorful strips of cotton cloth together to create skirts, blouses, and jackets. They traded this clothing for hand-operated sewing machines, and the designs became very distinctive.

By the 1920s, the women had developed the method of appliqué. They created unique patterns made of small pieces of cloth sewed together. The patterns are known by names such as thunder and lightning, fire, broken arrow, and tree.

Soon, the variety of designs and colors attracted tourists. They began to buy patchwork blouses, skirts, dresses, and jackets. Today, Seminole women make patchwork for their traditional clothing and to sell to tourists. The girl below is wearing a typical patchwork blouse.

they found in the swamps. They gathered in small villages and built chickees. They continued to practice the Green Corn Ceremony and lived much as they had before settlers came to Florida. They avoided the U.S. settlers who lived near them.

In the early 1900s, some Seminole began to trade again with U.S. citizens. Seminole trapped alligators, birds, and other animals. The alligator skins were used to make expensive shoes and handbags. The bird feathers were popular for women's hats. In return, the Seminole received pots and pans, bullets, and glass beads for jewelry. The Seminole also traded for cotton cloth, which they sewed into patterned skirts, blouses, and jackets. This patchwork clothing is the most famous of the Seminole crafts.

Around 1900, U.S. citizens began to drain the swamps to create more dry land for Florida's growing population. The citizens dug a series of canals. They changed the way water drained into the Everglades. As a result, swampland that the Seminole used became good farmland. The owners of the land sold it to U.S. settlers. The Seminole then had less land for their way of life.

To earn money, many Seminole depended on tourists to the Everglades. The Seminole showed tourists their chickees. They sold patchwork clothing, baskets, and dolls. They demonstrated how they cooked food, sewed patchwork, and made baskets from grass. They showed how they made canoes from cypress trees. They led hunting and fishing trips into the swamps.

In 1934, the U.S. Congress passed the Indian Reorganization Act. This law allowed American Indians to govern themselves under their own laws. In 1938, Congress set aside 80,000 acres (32,000 hectares) for the Seminole. These reservations were in Big Cypress Swamp and near Brighton and Hollywood, Florida. Later Florida reservations were added at Immokalee, Tampa, and Fort Pierce. Congress recognized the Seminole Tribe of Florida in 1957. The Miccosukee Seminole created their own tribe in 1962. They host the Music and Crafts Festival every summer in the Everglades.

Today, the Seminole Tribe of Florida owns more than 90,000 acres (36,000 hectares) of Florida land. They own orange groves, cattle ranches, hotels, and casinos. They have their own newspaper, school, museum, and airplane factory. The Florida Seminole have preserved their unique culture.

The Seminole Nation of Oklahoma

In the 1830s, the Seminole started to arrive in Indian Territory. They found that separate lands had not been set aside for them. They were forced to share a reservation with the Muskogee, who had helped the U.S. Army hunt Seminole in Florida. Many Seminole believed that the Muskogee were

their enemies and did not want to live with them. But the Seminole had no choice. For 20 years, the two tribes lived unhappily on the same reservation.

In 1856, the United States and the Muskogee signed a treaty to give the Seminole a separate reservation. The Seminole created the Seminole Nation of Oklahoma. The

A Florida Seminole farmer clears land for a sugarcane field. Many Seminole use machinery to help with farming.

U.S. government recognized the nation as independent. These Seminole built a capital city called Green Head Prairie, and Chief John Jumper governed them. They began to rebuild their culture and way of life in the West.

When the U.S. Civil War (1861–1865) began, the Seminole were divided. Most were loyal to the Northern

Chief John Jumper was the first leader of the Seminole Nation of Oklahoma.

states, but some fought for the Southern states. The Seminole also fought against each other and against the Cherokee and Choctaw.

When the Northern states won the war, the U.S. government punished the Seminole for joining the Southern states. The government forced them to sell their reservation to the United States and buy land from the Muskogee. The Seminole left Green Head Prairie and established a new capital at Wewoka, Oklahoma. By 1868, many Seminole had gathered on their new reservation homeland.

In 1897, the Seminole agreed to split their reservation. Individual Seminole could sell land that they did not need for their families. By 1920, the Seminole owned only one-fifth of the original 200,000 acres (81,000 hectares). They had to buy land from the Muskogee nation so everyone had enough.

Today, the Seminole Nation of Oklahoma consists of 14 tribal bands who live in their own towns. There are 12 Native Indian bands and two bands of Freedmen. Each town has its own rules and elects its own chairman and vice chairman. Each band sends two representatives to the Tribal Council. The council is responsible for job development, social programs, and business decisions. The Florida Seminole and the Oklahoma Seminole work to preserve their traditional way of life.

Young Seminole children display their traditional patchwork clothing.

Chapter Five

Sharing the Traditions

The Florida and Oklahoma Seminole continue to practice parts of their traditional religion. Although many Seminole have become Christians, groups in Florida and Oklahoma still celebrate the Green Corn Ceremony. The two nations have lived separately for more than 100 years, so individual ceremonies and dances are somewhat different for each tribe.

In the 1940s, the Seminole Tribe of Florida established the Ahfachkee Indian School. It began in a chickee and offered classes through fourth grade. Today, the school educates Seminole children from kindergarten through 12th grade. It teaches Seminole languages and history.

The Seminole and Miccosukee Tribes of Florida still use two native languages and English. Some speak only Muskogee, and others speak only Miccosukee. A few Seminole speak both languages.

The Florida Seminole live mainly on or near their reservations. This location allows the older members to teach the young people about traditional culture and language. In 1997, the Seminole opened the Ah-Tah-Thi-Ki Museum on Big Cypress Reservation to preserve their history and educate people about the Seminole.

The crafts of patchwork, basketmaking, and doll making continue in Florida. Tourists buy these Seminole crafts. Some Seminole artists are able to earn a living by selling their crafts. Some older Seminole worry that tourism, TV, and other modern ways of life will make the young Seminole forget their culture. But the leaders of the Seminole Tribe of Florida are committed to teaching the culture and crafts to their children.

In Oklahoma, about 60 percent of the Seminole live in Seminole County. Oil is an important natural resource for their area, and many businesses in Wewoka provide services and materials to oil companies. The rest of the Oklahoma

Betty Mae Jumper

Betty Mae Jumper was born Betty Mae Tiger in 1923 in a small village called Indiantown in the Everglades. Her mother was a Seminole, and her father was a French fur trapper. Her mother spoke no English. Betty Mae grew up on the Hollywood Reservation, where she learned English, Muskogee, and Miccosukee. At age 14, Betty Mae attended a boarding school in Cherokee, North Carolina. In 1945, she became the first Seminole to graduate from high school.

After high school, Betty Mae moved to Oklahoma and studied to become a nurse. When she returned to Florida, she married Moses Jumper and worked to improve health services for the Seminole. In 1967, she was elected as the chairperson of the Florida Seminole. She is the only Seminole woman ever to hold this position. In 1997, the Florida Commission on the Status of Women named her Woman of the Year. Seminole stories have interested Betty Mae since she was a child. She collected stories from Seminole storytellers and wrote a book called *The Legends of the Seminole*. The stories teach important lessons about life and nature. Betty Mae is well known in Florida for her skills as a storyteller. She lives on the Hollywood and Big Cypress Reservations in Florida.

Seminole have moved to other cities in Oklahoma and across the United States to find jobs.

Every September, the Seminole Days Festival is held at Mekasukey Mission Tribal Grounds near Seminole,

A student learns how to make Seminole beadwork from teacher Teresa Jumper at a Seminole school.

Oklahoma. This celebration is open to other Indian nations and to tourists. It attracts Seminole from across the country for stomp dances and historical plays. Many people take part in stickball games and other sporting events.

Preserving Their Ways

The Seminole want their children to know their own traditions as well as the ways of other Americans. They want their children to have a chance to be successful in life.

Many young people do not speak their native language well. Many have moved away from home to attend college or look for jobs. Some older Seminole fear that the language and traditions may disappear if the young people leave home. For this reason, older members have begun to teach Seminole traditions in the native language. For instance, leaders of the Oklahoma Seminole want the Muskogee language to be taught in Oklahoma public schools along with English.

The Seminole have fought hard to maintain their culture and traditions. They fought three wars that changed their culture forever. Many were forced to move to Indian Territory, a land different from their Florida lands. Yet the Seminole tribes continue to work to preserve their traditions, languages, and culture for the future.

Seminole Timeline

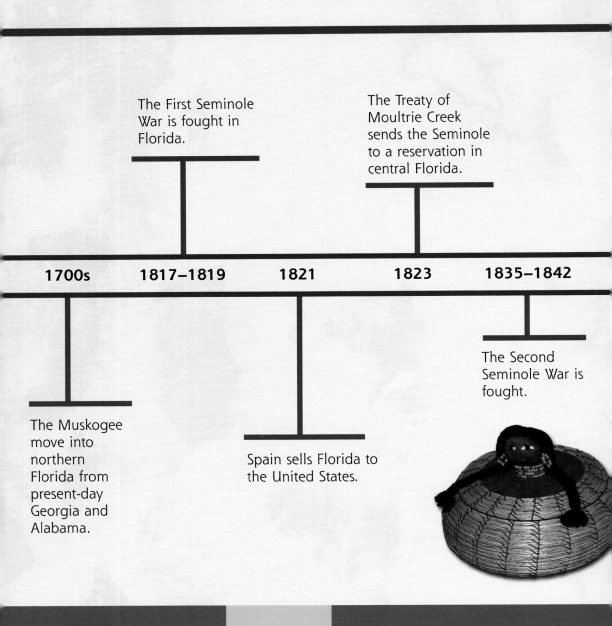

The First Seminole War is fought in Florida.

The Treaty of Moultrie Creek sends the Seminole to a reservation in central Florida.

1700s   1817–1819   1821   1823   1835–1842

The Second Seminole War is fought.

The Muskogee move into northern Florida from present-day Georgia and Alabama.

Spain sells Florida to the United States.

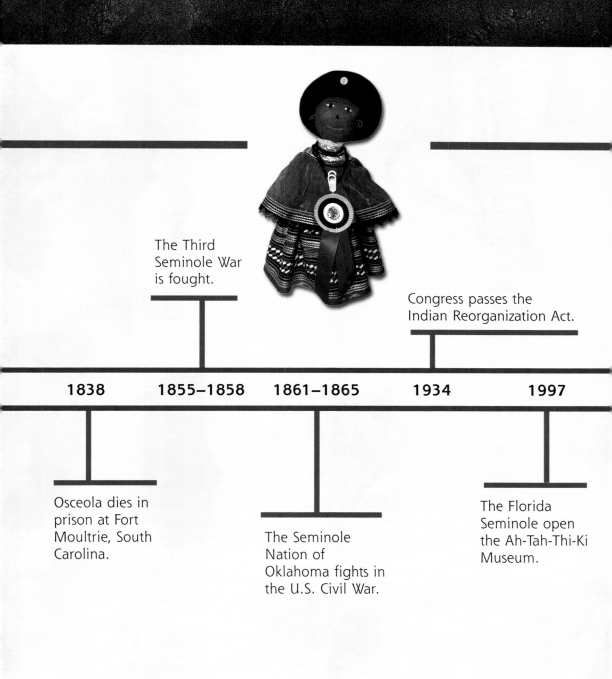

The Third
Seminole War
is fought.

Congress passes the
Indian Reorganization Act.

| 1838 | 1855–1858 | 1861–1865 | 1934 | 1997 |

Osceola dies in
prison at Fort
Moultrie, South
Carolina.

The Seminole
Nation of
Oklahoma fights in
the U.S. Civil War.

The Florida
Seminole open
the Ah-Tah-Thi-Ki
Museum.

Glossary

ancestor (AN-sess-tur)—a member of a person's family who lived a long time ago

chickee (CHIK-ee)—a Seminole home with open sides and a roof of palmetto leaves

clan (KLAN)—a large group of related families

Everglades (EV-ur-glaydz)—a large, swampy area of south Florida

Freedmen (FREED-men)—escaped African American slaves who lived with the Seminole in Florida and Oklahoma

Muskogee (muh-SKOH-gee)—people who later became the Seminole nation

reservation (rez-ur-VAY-shuhn)—land that the U.S. government sets aside for an American Indian nation to use

For Further Reading

Bial, Raymond. *The Seminole.* Lifeways. New York: Benchmark Books, 2000.

Girod, Christina M. *Native Americans of the Southeast.* Indigenous Peoples of North America. San Diego: Lucent Books, 2001.

Kavasch, E. Barrie. *The Seminoles.* Indian Nations. Austin, Tex.: Raintree Steck-Vaughn, 2000.

Places to Write and Visit

Ah-Tah-Thi-Ki Museum
HC-61
P.O. Box 21-A
Clewiston, FL 33440

Seminole Nation Museum
524 South Wewoka Avenue
P.O. Box 532
Wewoka, OK 74884

The Seminole Tribe of Florida
6300 Stirling Road
Hollywood, FL 33024

Internet Sites

Native Peoples Arts and Lifeways Magazine: Recipes—Florida Powwow Food
http://www.nativepeoples.com/np_features/np_recipes/winter97_recipe.html

Seminole Nation of Oklahoma
http://www.cowboy.net/native/seminole

The Seminole Tribe of Florida

http://www.seminoletribe.com

Index